Mau-Mauing the Media

South African Institute of Race Relations
Current Publications

Monica Bot, *The Blackboard Debate: Hurdles, Options and Opportunities in School Integration* (1991)
W J P Carr, *Soweto: Its Creation, Life and Decline* (1990)
Joseph Kelly, *Finding a Cure: The Politics of Health in South Africa* (1990)
Stanley Mogoba, *Harmony, the Key to National Reconstruction* (1990)
John Kane-Berman et al, *Beating Apartheid and Building the Future* (1990)
Harry Mashabela, *Mekhukhu: Urban African Cities of the Future* (1990)
John Kane-Berman, *South Africa's Silent Revolution* (1990)
Colleen McCaul, *No Easy Ride: The Rise and Future of the Black Taxi Industry* (1990)
Justice M M Corbertt, *Guaranteeing Fundamental Freedoms in a New South Africa* (1990)
Mauritz Moolman, *From Town to Township: Regional Services Councils Assessed* (1990)
Steven Friedman, *Options for the Future: Government Reform Strategy and Prospects for Structural Change* (1990)
Paul Hendler, *Paths to Power* (1989)
Stanley Mogoba, *A New Africa* (1989)
Stanley Mogoba, John Kane-Berman and Ronnie Bethlehem, *Sanctions and the Alternatives* (2nd edition, 1989)
Harry Mashabela and Monty Narsoo, *The Boksburg Boycott* (1989)
Paul Hendler, *Politics on the Home Front* (1989)
Steven Friedman and Monty Narsoo, *A New Mood in Moscow: Soviet Attitudes to South Africa* (1989)
Harry Mashabela, *Fragile Figures: The 1988 PWV Township Elections* (1989)
Harry Mashabela, *Townships of the PWV* (1989)
Paul Hendler, *Urban Policy and Housing* (1988)
Monica Bot, *Training on Separate Tracks* (1988)

These are available from:

The Publications Department
South African Institute of Race Relations
P O Box 31044
Braamfontein
2017 South Africa

Mau-Mauing the Media: New Censorship for the New South Africa

Thami Mazwai
Arthur Konigkramer
Connie Molusi
Kaizer Nyatsumba
Dawn Lindberg
Lionel Abrahams
Nomavenda Mathiane
Joe Thloloe
John Kane-Berman

SOUTH AFRICAN INSTITUTE OF RACE RELATIONS
JOHANNESBURG
1991

Published by the South African Institute of Race Relations
Auden House, 68 De Korte Street,
Braamfontein, Johannesburg, 2001 South Africa

© South African Institute of Race Relations, 1991

ISBN 0-86982-393-0   PD7/91

Members of the media are free to reprint or report information, either in whole or in part, contained in this publication on the strict understanding that the South African Institute of Race Relations is acknowledged.
    Otherwise, no part of this publication may be reproduced, stored in a retrieval system or transmitted in any form or by any means, electrical, mechanical, photocopy, recording or otherwise, without the prior permission of the publisher.

Printed by Galvin & Sales, Cape Town

MAU-MAUING THE MEDIA: NEW CENSORSHIP FOR THE NEW SOUTH AFRICA

EXECUTIVE SUMMARY

During the last few years, in discussions held at the South African Institute of Race Relations, black journalists estimated that roughly 60 per cent of what was happening in the country did not reach the press. They indicated they were being subjected to an unofficial form of censorship, perpetrated by political activists, that was largely unrecognised and unreported. They described the risks journalists took if they wrote about 'sensitive issues' — uncomfortable issues that many people believed should not be raised in public.

In August 1990 the Institute invited five senior black journalists, a leading writer and critic, the managing director of the only black-owned newspaper, and one of the country's best known entertainers, to a seminar at which the kinds of problems and events that do not receive sufficient media coverage could be told to a wider audience of Institute members. This book contains transcripts of the talks and discussions at that seminar.

Speakers frequently referred to 'certain organisations', which was a chilling indication of the ferocity of the unwritten pressures to which writers, journalists and artists have been subjected during the years of unrest and mass mobilisation in South Africa. It became apparent during the seminar that those who are brave enough to resist these pressures do not receive the support that was afforded to writers and politicians who fell foul of state censorship in the days of granite apartheid. As one speaker said, when the government detained or arrested a journalist, he or she 'became a hero in the people's eyes', but that was not the case when political organisations took action against a reporter.

According to another speaker, 'We have a situation in which journalists are far less exposed to arrest, detention and incarceration by the government than they used to be, but are being threatened and manhandled by political activists in the townships, in the towns and everywhere, and are being told to toe the line or else.'

The seminar was told that criticising strategies such as class boycotts was considered taboo by political activists. A boycott of the *Sowetan* had been announced, for example, after one of the newspaper's journalists had been accused of publishing a story that 'sowed division'. In Natal, the circulation of the Inkatha-owned newspaper, *Ilanga*, dropped by as much as 23 000 after shopkeepers who sold it were attacked and people who were caught reading it were forced to eat it and sometimes threatened with death.

A theme that emerged during the seminar was a feeling among black journalists that they had been hampered by white liberals in their attempts to be even-handed in their reporting. Several of them commented that white liberals and journalists seemed reluctant to criticise any actions or strategies that emanated from black leaders and their organisations for fear of having their liberal credentials questioned. One of the speakers mentioned the example of the Anti-Censorship Action Group, which cited as instances of censorship 'a surprising range of phenomena' (including police action during protest marches and right-wing disruption of meetings) but maintained a silence over the ANC's selective cultural boycott.

The seminar heard repeated reports of coercion and intimidation in the townships. A senior labour and political journalist, formerly publications officer of the National Council of Trade Unions, attributed the current political intolerance to the period popularly known as the mass insurrection era spanning 1984 to 1986, when a culture of 'people's war' was born, with compulsory attendance at street committees and cruel punishment for disobedience. He said, 'I find it interesting that people have resorted to the very tactics they so strenuously criticised when it was the state that used them', and he added, 'the sooner people stand up courageously to challenge undemocratic political practices the better, otherwise there is no future for this country, this country is doomed.'

Another speaker described how organisations and meetings set up by black parents to resolve the education crisis were 'hijacked' by political groups who favoured continued disruption in the schools, and she spoke of the helplessness of parents attempting to deal with this.

On a more hopeful note, one speaker said she believed the ANC cultural desk had become aware of the dangers of censorship of the mind and were trying hard to move away from that kind of dictatorship. In discussion, however, another speaker disagreed and described how *Tribute* magazine had recently been threatened with boycott for publishing interviews he had conducted with musicians who had uncomplimentary things to say about the cultural desk.

When Mrs Helen Suzman asked whether anything could be done to mobilise the vast majority of people who wanted to live stable lives but who seemed to be 'totally intimidated and overcome', the Institute's Executive Director, Mr John Kane-Berman, said, 'This seminar is part of the answer — making the information we have been given today more widely available.' He added that an important part of the Institute's work over the last 61 years had been to 'expose things to the light of day' in order to encourage people to take action to rectify them. One thing the Institute could do was set an example by resisting pressures to conform to the dictates of political organisations or toe any particular line. Referring to the concluding comments made by the Institute's president, the Rev Dr Stanley Mogoba, who chaired the seminar, Mr Kane-Berman said, 'Dr Mogoba says that this audience has been shocked by what it has heard today. I am glad to hear it: that was the intention.'

Contents

Executive summary v

1. The present and future role of the press 11
   *Thami Mazwai, Senior Assistant Editor
   and Business Editor, Sowetan*

2. The new censorship 19
   *Arthur Konigkramer, Managing Director
   Mandla-Matla Publishing, owners of Ilanga*

3. What hope political pluralism in South Africa? 25
   Connie Molusi, journalist at SAPA

4. Whither black art? The cultural desks 29
   *Kaizer Nyatsumba, poet, writer,
   senior political journalist on The Star*

5. Censorship 39
   *Dawn Lindberg, theatre producer
   and entertainer*

6. Time to speak out 43
   Lionel Abrahams, writer, poet, publisher

7. The Soweto schools 45
   *Nomavenda Mathiane, author and
   Assistant Editor of Frontline*

8. The child masters 51
   Joe Thloloe, Assistant Editor, Sowetan

9. Discussion 55

10. What's to be done? 63
    *John Kane-Berman, Executive Director,
    South African Institute of
    Race Relations*

ix

1. THE PRESENT AND FUTURE ROLE OF THE PRESS

THAMI MAZWAI

Senior assistant editor and business editor, Sowetan

Little has been said about a new type of censorship that is around in the townships and poses the most powerful threat to press freedom in this country. We have a situation in which journalists are far less exposed to arrest, detention and incarceration by the government than they used to be, but are being threatened and manhandled by political activists in the townships, in the towns and everywhere, and are being told to toe the line 'or else'.

Now when you are told to toe the line, you must make your stories convey a particular meaning, in other words you must be a propagandist. You must play the numbers game. If there were twenty people at a meeting, and it is not in the interests of the organisation that called the meeting for the public to be told that there were twenty people present, you have got to add a couple of noughts, and if you don't add those couple of noughts then you become an enemy of the struggle.

A lot of us have been very sympathetic to some of these things, because of our commitment to the struggle, but the journalist in us has always forced us to try our level best to reject and ignore the pressures, and fight against them. Some have been successful in maintaining their credibility as journalists. Unfortunately not all of us have been able to do that. As a result, what appears in the newspapers, even today, will perhaps be 40% or 50% accurate, but there is that 50% which is made up of particular political positions, specific distortions and an attempt to influence the readership — the public — to think in a particular direction.

Brute force and money now play a dominant role in the townships. I will not give specific details, as it is not my brief for today, but we have a problem with a lot of organisations in the country, which will not fund a project for community development unless it is proposed by a particular political group. These organisations seem to think that people starve, or need assistance, only if they are of a particular political persuasion. If, for instance, you have a literacy project at the hostels, and the people who need money for that project are not of a specific political persuasion, then they are not likely to get any money, but if they are of the accepted persuasion, they will get more than they asked for. Student groups, if they are of a specific political persuasion, are given amounts like R20 000 to run an organisation. Knowing that 17-year-olds and 18-year-olds are in control of funds of this size, one can better understand what is now happening in the townships. And R20 000 is a very conservative estimate: the number commonly cited is R40 000. You have some of these youngsters driving around in cars, with loads and loads of money in their pockets, and when you try and find out where they got it, you discover it comes from a certain overseas funding organisation. There are countries that are particularly guilty of this, and I am not going to mention them, but I believe that they have done a great disservice to the struggle in this country: they have created a monster that has now become uncontrollable.

What I saw overseas in this connection was just shameful. I was there at a time when there was a lot of protest against the convictions of the Sharpeville Six. I was at a meeting where somebody from the anti-apartheid movement was going to be a speaker, as well as somebody from the black consciousness movement, and I was also asked if I was available to speak. But then there were objections that the guy from the black consciousness movement, from AZAPO [the Azanian People's Organisation], was not qualified to speak at this meeting – this guy was from inside the country and knew more about the Sharpeville Six than anybody else, but the anti-apartheid movement would not allow him to speak because AZAPO is regarded as one of the organisations that are not with the struggle, regardless of the fact that we still have AZAPO people being detained. The same thing happened with me: fortunately I had anticipated it, and said I was not available to speak, but emotions were already being whipped up to prevent me from speaking. Yet as a journalist whose newspaper had been covering the plight of the Sharpeville Six, I believe I was more than qualified to speak on this issue. The problem was that my political credentials were not kosher, and instead they got somebody from the anti-apartheid movement, who had never been to South Africa, to speak on the Sharpeville Six.

This is what has been happening overseas, and a lot of it has been happening in this country right down to the grassroots. It permeates to the youngsters, to the activists, to the unions, where you find that everybody believes that this particular ideology is the ideology that must be supported. It also happens in the many companies that are setting up welfare projects: they make sure they have people of a particular ideology as trustees. If you belong to a rival ideology you are elbowed out because your politics don't qualify you to decide on projects in the townships.

We have now reached a point where the journalist is told, 'You are either for us or against us.' It is sheer political blackmail. Many of us have been in jail several times, and we don't mind going to jail if it is in pursuit of what we believe in. I am a journalist and have been one since 1969, and I don't think I am going to write distortion simply because a law has been passed by the government. I will take whatever risk I can to make sure that the public knows what is happening. But here is this new threat: not only do I have to defy the government, I also have to present the facts in such a way that I am seen to be pushing a particular organisation. Many of us have said we simply cannot have this.

Now to give you another aspect of the scenario, let us have a look at the schools. This is one area that black journalists are very reluctant to cover. The school situation in the townships, to be frank, is out of control. Matrics are supposed to be writing examinations, but I don't know how many of them have even done two months of reading this year. They have not been able to do any reading because of the perpetual class boycotts and teacher 'chalkdowns'. I am solidly behind any struggle against bantu education, but I simply will not have the type of campaign that cuts off one's nose to spite one's face, because in the final analysis the people who suffer are the children, not anybody else. It is these children who will have to slot themselves into a new South Africa, and I don't believe that the new South Africa will be able to afford to have illiterates in important positions. So we are still going to have white rule in the new South Africa, not because of skin colour, but because whites will be the only people qualified to fill certain positions. Very ironic!

We also have in the schools a situation where last year's dropouts lead this year's class boycotts. The argument is simple: if I didn't attend school last year, why should others attend school this year? The process repeats itself every year.

Unfortunately those people who are at the forefront of the schools crisis do not, I believe, have the interests of our children, or the country, at heart. This is a very serious allegation to make, an allegation one would not dare publish in a newspaper. We have so many chiefs who are running the show that each and every one of them has got to make sure he comes with a campaign of his own, and when he does, there is this ready army of youths to carry it out. They are told they are working for the liberation of their country.

And then we have the type of duplicity where certain leaders, adult people themselves, some of them qualified, will organise class boycotts in Soweto but send their children to private schools in town; in other words the child who suffers is the child of that Soweto auntie who cannot afford the fees for private school. Some of the leaders are even fortunate enough to have their children's school fees paid by one of the many foundations with conscience money to dispense. This is the situation that you find in the townships, but if a journalist dares highlight it, he is seen not as giving facts, but as being 'against the struggle'. It would take a lot of journalists with a lot of guts to write about this, because if you are seen to be against the struggle, normally you are not denounced at a public meeting. The weapon being used is to whisper, to spread the word around that 'so-and-so is against the struggle'. Heaven help you should you ever be cornered by youngsters: they will make you pay for being against the struggle.

We also have cases of complete takeover of certain schools by student organisations. If a school has been taken over by students belonging to a particular organisation, students belonging to rival organisations are thrown out completely, they are hounded out and told not to set foot in that school unless they are prepared to embrace the ideology of the group in control. One can go on and on with this type of scenario, but I don't think we have the time for that.

When we come to the question of democracy in the townships, let us not fool ourselves: there is no democracy in the townships, and the type of decision-making that goes on there is a question of what I think is good for you, not what you think is good for yourself. We also have a lot of that in the unions, where overseas organisations are pumping money into certain unions as long as they pursue a specific line. The unions that are getting money then take it upon themselves to hammer other unions out of existence. We have had a lot of killings and petrol bombings, a lot of union-splitting, and it has all been a traumatic experience. I was in the unions and I know what I am talking about. I was treasurer of MWASA [the Media Workers' Association of South Africa] for about five years, and I know what pressures we were subjected to because our organisation refused to adopt a political document on the grounds that we are basically a worker organisation and our workers come from all ideologies.

Now this is the atmosphere that you find in the townships, that you find in the country, that you find in Johannesburg. This is the type of scenario that exists today where you have a fight between Inkatha and the ANC. I am not saying both organisations are innocent; we have a lot of political intolerance on both sides. These organisations are quick to talk about freedom of association, but when you try to put that into effect you find that there is no freedom of association whatsoever.

Reporters in Natal say they are having difficulty practising their profession: one night Inkatha people will come to them saying, 'Look, we don't like what you are writing,' and then the next night people from the ANC or the UDF will come and say, 'Look, we don't like what you are writing,' and in the end they feel like saying, 'I have had enough,' and getting out.

Lastly, something that I think we should perhaps bring up: a few years ago there was a campaign for the boycott of the *Sowetan*, a boycott that was called, I think, by the people who believed in press freedom. That was a very traumatic experience. I was at the *Sowetan* at the time. I was the news editor and we were being accused of being anti a specific political organisation. Obviously there was no truth in that allegation. What happened was that I got a visit from some prominent activists who said, 'Your newspaper is the only one writing about the PAC and AZAPO. Why are you giving life to organisations that don't exist?' My response was, 'We are reporting on meetings being held by these organisations, and if at all you say they don't exist, what about the people who attend those meetings? Are you saying that we should not report on those meetings?' They said, 'It is only a few people going there.' I said, 'The same number of people go to your meetings as go to these meetings, if not the same people.' They said, 'But you are dividing the oppressed. We must only have one organisation.' So I said, 'Who decides on this one organisation?' There was a lot of mumbling and grumbling and they left, and the *Sowetan* continued publishing stories about the ANC, the PAC, and the black consciousness movement. I don't believe that even as news editor or senior assistant editor I have the right to decide which organisation is acceptable. I believe that that is the right of the reader, the individual. When we took that position at the *Sowetan* a lot of sentiments were aroused against the newspaper in the community, so it was not surprising that a press conference was held to announce a boycott of the *Sowetan*.

Three months before this there had been other pressures on all black journalists, and we set up what we called an 'eminent persons group' consisting of one representative from each newspaper, to go and talk to a certain political organisation. I remember at the *Sowetan* we had Themba Molefe who is now at the *Detroit News*; he's just there for six months. There was somebody from every newspaper except *The Weekly Mail* and *New Nation*. When we asked *New Nation* why they had no representative on this committee to stop the conflict and the pressure on black journalists, they said they did not have such a problem. *The Weekly Mail* had a similar attitude. So the newspapers that had to fight this battle were the mainstream newspapers, reporters from *The Star*, *City Press* and so on.

At a meeting held at the South African Council of Churches, one of the activists said, 'Three people, at the *Sowetan* and *The Star*, are the problem. If you don't deal with those people we are going to ban all of you.'

So we had these pressures on the *Sowetan*, including an attempt to necklace one of our reporters* — thankfully we have never had a necklacing of a journalist — and a petrol bomb was thrown at the home of another journalist. This was in 1984. Our current news editor could not come to work one day because the local youngsters in the township called him to a meeting. Here were 13-year-olds who could hardly spell their names questioning a journalist on the policy of his newspaper. He could have said anything — they would not have known the difference — but you see, this was the type of pressure that was being exerted on us.

We used to get calls at night in which we were told what some people thought of us. One night I got a telephone call (Jon Qwelane got a similar call) to say I was going to be attacked, and I had to take my wife and children away to my mother's place, so that if these people came, then whatever happened to me, my children would not be exposed to it. But I certainly was not going to leave my house, because that would have been a sign of weakness on my part.

Now these are the pressures that exist, and we have them on a day-to-day basis. You are not allowed to say, 'This is what happened.' I am not talking of comment, I am not talking about thinking. If you do say, 'This is what happened,' you must make sure that it does not reflect badly on a political organisation. This is the type of pressure that is creating a problem for the future press in this country.

We at the *Sowetan* have started a campaign for a free press because we believe that freedom is indivisible. Freedom cannot be applied at

---

* See *Race Relations News*, vol 52 no 1, April 1990, p13

one level while at another level we have suppression; freedom has got to span all human activities. You have got to have cultural freedom, press freedom, economic freedom, freedom in all respects, because freedom guarantees the individual his humanity. This is what I believe we should address ourselves to as we move towards this new South Africa. We are going to face tremendous problems, I know that, but I believe that there is a core of journalists who would lay their lives on the line to protect your right to know. We don't believe that press censorship is evil only when it is perpetrated by the government, but also when it is applied by black organisations. We believe any suppression of information is evil whether it is done by a black government or a white government, the more so when it is done by organisations which themselves maintain that they are fighting for the liberation of our people. What freedom are we talking about if we are going to be told, 'This is how to think'? That is not my job as a journalist. I am not here to come and tell you what to think or how to think. I am merely here to give you the information on which to make whatever decisions you have to make on any one day.

2. THE NEW CENSORSHIP

ARTHUR KONIGKRAMER

Managing Director Mandla-Matla Publishing, owners of Ilanga

I would like to say a little more about who I actually work for, because I think it is important for objectivity that I do so. Our newspaper is owned by a company called Mandla-Matla Publishing, and the sole shareholder of that company is Inkatha. I should also like to say at the outset that I disagree with the assertion that political parties should not be allowed to own newspapers. If one subscribes to a belief in a free press, then I believe anybody has the right to own a newspaper.

Ilanga was formed in 1903 by Dr John Dube, who was the first president of what is now the African National Congress. During the 1950s the paper was taken over by white business interests, and it remained in white hands until 1 April 1987 when it was taken over from the Argus company by Inkatha. It thus became the first major African newspaper in modern times to be wholly owned by black South Africans. Our company is opposed to any form of racism and accordingly the race of the owners shouldn't really be an issue, but I think the reality after 80 years of total exclusion of Africans from the political process and, to a large degree, from the free enterprise system, dictates that *Ilanga*'s acquisition by black people is not without significance. When I agreed to join *Ilanga* in April 1987 I was appointed general manager of Mandla-Matla Publishing. It was a limited liability company and had been formed to take over the newspaper. The board of directors was headed by Dr Oscar Dhlomo, former secretary general of Inkatha, and all the other directors had very close links with either the KwaZulu government or Inkatha. In November 1987 the president of Inkatha, Dr Mangosuthu Buthelezi, restructured the board of directors. The purpose of this move was to remove all people with links to the KwaZulu administration, or to Inkatha, from the board. The former president of the Black Community Programmes, Mr Bill Bhengu, the attorney, who has now died, was appointed chairman, and I was appointed managing director. I think that was a fairly significant event and a fairly significant political statement. Both the board and the shareholders approved and published editorial policy guidelines. Again I think that is something which is not taken note of sufficiently. I know of no other newspaper which has done that in recent times. My time does not allow me to spell them out in detail, so I shall confine myself to what I consider to be the most important policy guideline, and this is that the company would place South Africa's wellbeing above all else. To this end *Ilanga* would adhere to independent and honest standards of journalism that did not pander to personal and sectional interests but are concerned solely with the public interest.

Events surrounding the takeover of *Ilanga* by Inkatha deserve brief mention, because they were a precursor to actions that form the basis of our discussions today. When the takeover was announced on 15 February 1987, there was an outcry from the editorial staff, from the South African Society of Journalists (SASJ) and from a large array of politicians on the left. The bulk of the staff signed a press statement condemning the sale, saying that they would not work for the new company.

The actual takeover was on 15 April 1987. On Thursday 16 April the entire editorial staff refused to work. Few people believed that Inkatha would be able to produce a newspaper without a single member of the editorial staff.

Much to everybody's surprise the newspaper appeared on the streets on the morning of 21 April. On the afternoon of 21 April the editor and assistant editor returned to *Ilanga*'s office and said that they were prepared to work for the new company. Later the same day the rest of the staff arrived in the company of SASJ officials and attempted to stage a sit-in clearly designed to block any further issues of the newspaper, and they were ordered out of the building by Dr Dhlomo. Still on the same day, four of the next most senior members of staff arrived at *Ilanga* and said that they too would be prepared to work for the new company. The six were re-employed there and then. The remaining 20 members of staff were retrenched at great cost and after protracted negotiations, in fact, I might say, the cost nearly broke us.

Serious intimidation designed to block the sales of the next issue of *Ilanga* (22 April) began on 22 April 1987. Shopkeepers were threatened that their shops would be burnt down if they stocked *Ilanga*, the lives of former *Ilanga* staff who had joined Mandla-Matla were threatened, and their homes had to be protected by police. Threats soon followed against the new staff members. These staff members were not from the Durban area, they'd been brought in from all over the place, and we were forced to put them up in hotels in Durban to ensure their safety as they could not go into the townships. The old staff who had joined were prevented from coming to work, leaving a new, completely inexperienced staff to produce the issue of 7 May 1987.

Numerous bomb threats were received at *Ilanga*, causing white staff employed by Natal Newspapers to become very nervous. That also almost led to a breakdown, because Natal Newspapers (which is part of the Argus group) had a management agreement in terms of which they sold the advertising. So with these threats most of the staff actually walked out and it became problematical to run the newspaper.

Although sales dropped marginally because of the intimidation, the campaign fizzled out after about six weeks. I believe there were two main reasons for this. Firstly, the takeover of *Ilanga* by a black company. I think the bulk of the people recognised that as a fairly significant event. It generated discussion and people wanted to know what was going on, and so they bought the paper. Secondly, it became apparent that buyers resorted to the expedient of switching from buying *Ilanga* in the townships to buying it in the streets of Durban. Just a digression here, to show you how violent the situation became. Many people who were caught buying *Ilanga* in the townships were actually forced to eat the paper — it was stuffed into their mouths. These are the sort of things that happened.

From there on, as I said, the campaign tapered off. During the first year in which we controlled the company, which was 1987, circulation grew by an average of 11% per month, and during the second financial year growth actually reached 18% per month. By January 1989 *Ilanga*'s circulation had reached a figure of 144 054, which is a very dramatic increase — 42% up on the January 1987 figure of 101 098 when we took it over. In February 1989 the circulation reached a new record of 147 767. This figure was improved on slightly in September 1989 when sales reached 147 854. I believe we can modestly claim that these figures were testimony to our company's professionalism, and I think, more importantly, they were actually proof positive that we were producing a better newspaper, a paper that the reading public obviously enjoyed and wanted, and I think that's why the numbers increased steadily.

But, Mr Chairman, the political opponents of our shareholder were obviously also watching our growth very carefully, and they didn't like what they saw. Signs of fresh intimidation, designed to block *Ilanga*'s sales, began to appear towards the end of 1989. Initially it did not meet with much success, but it grew steadily worse from April this year.

Shopkeepers in Umlazi, KwaMashu, Edendale and Mpumalanga have been intimidated into not selling *Ilanga*. Vans entering Umlazi were often turned back if copies of *Ilanga* were inside. However, the faceless intimidators allowed the vans through with copies of *Umafrika*, a newspaper fiercely critical of Inkatha and a strong supporter of the ANC. It is owned by the Catholic church and it is financed with funds exclusively drawn from outside South Africa. Our newspaper has no foreign funding, it is funded entirely on its own, it has no handouts given to it.

Shopkeepers were intimidated into not selling *Ilanga*, but at the same time they were encouraged to sell *Umafrika* and as a consequence the sales of that newspaper have risen sharply—and I think it is very significant that nobody has sought to intimidate shopkeepers into not selling *Umafrika*. Natal Newspapers, publishers of both *Ilanga* and *Umafrika*, reported to us on 26 April that a total of ten agents in Umlazi had asked for the suspension of supplies of *Ilanga*. The same day they reported to us that two outlets in KwaMashu had also said they no longer wished to sell the paper. Again on the same day, that is 26 April, three major outlets in the Edendale area of Pietermaritzburg also stopped selling *Ilanga*. On 3 May this year, Natal Newspapers reported in writing that one of their drivers had been confronted by four men in Umlazi. Two of them produced handguns, and told the driver, 'You will finish to read *Ilanga* in Umlazi.' They took the keys away, and drove off with the van with many thousands of copies of *Ilanga* and it has never been recovered. On the same day a further 17 of the 22 remaining outlets in the Edendale area of Pietermaritzburg also stopped selling *Ilanga*, and in Durban an Indian shopkeeper also stopped selling it. The reason I mention this case is that it was the first outlet outside the black townships that stopped selling *Ilanga*, and it was as a result of threats. From as far afield as Piet Retief on the Transvaal border we got reports that people who were buying *Ilanga* were quickly folding it into a small package and hiding it in their pockets so that it couldn't be seen.

But during July this year an even more sinister development started in the heart of Durban. People buying the newspaper at street corners in Smith and West Streets were followed by unknown individuals. The papers were confiscated and the buyers were threatened with death if they were seen with the paper again. Those responsible had clearly also cottoned on to the switch in buying patterns and they decided to plug the loopholes. As I indicated, people had started buying their copies of *Ilanga* in the streets of Durban. This is very clearly what some people were trying to stop.

I think I should give you the figures so that you can see how dramatically this affected us. Average sales for February (1990) stood at 146 890; they dropped to 133 104 in March and 123 514 in April, so we had a drop of about 23 000 copies. The sales figures for the same three months in 1989 were: 147 767, 135 180 and 146 128, just by way of comparison to show that it wasn't a seasonal thing, that in fact there was a very dramatic drop. In May this year, average sales per issue went even lower, down to 121 966 compared to 138 632 for May the previous year. In June the sales dropped even lower to 120 232, compared to 138 632 for the same month in 1989. Just by way of parenthesis I would like to mention that *Umafrika* sales soared from 9 955 in June last year to over 53 296 for the same period this year. I think you can see what was actually happening there.

Thankfully there are now signs that the campaign to depress *Ilanga* sales is beginning to lose momentum; sales have again begun to climb despite the fact that many previous outlets still do not stock *Ilanga*. We are confident that we will see steady growth during the next month and that we will soon, hopefully by the end of the year, be back to where we were at round about 147 000.

Now I want to deal very briefly with threats against the lives of *Ilanga* staff. These have also been made very consistently, mainly since the beginning of this year. Basically there were three staff members involved, the most serious threats being made against me personally, I presume that is because I run the company. Callers claiming to be members of Umkhonto we Sizwe twice telephoned the editor of *Ilanga* during this month and threatened to blow up our building. At the height of the campaign my life was threatened about three times a week, mostly by telephone. Prowlers began to visit my home at night and regularly triggered an alarm system that we had installed. One individual actually went through the tiled roof while jumping from the garage to the main house, and as a consequence of that we have been forced to employ armed guards to protect the building. During the second week of August anonymous callers threatened to assassinate my younger brother, who works for the provincial administration, and the threat was directly linked to my working at *Ilanga*.

But threats and intimidation are not the style of the left alone. When I joined *Ilanga* in 1973 (and that was when the Argus company still owned it), it was a newspaper that hardly ever dealt with political issues, in fact it was a decidedly yellow newspaper. I found it quite distasteful and I set out to change this, and it was not long before the newspaper began to attract the attention of right-wing agents of the state. I was threatened regularly and the tyres of my car were slashed twice. What was really upsetting at that time was that my father, who was a fairly old man, was visited (obviously, I must presume) by agents of the right, and they told him if he knew what was good for me he would make sure that I disappeared from *Ilanga*.

Mr Chairman, I would just like to make a few brief observations in conclusion. I believe that whatever *Ilanga*'s sins in the eyes of those who have sought to prevent others from reading it, it cannot be gainsaid that it is catering adequately for the information needs of a very large and growing number of people. In fact, it is read now by between 1,6 and 2 million readers.

You will have noticed from what I have told you that the campaign against us really began to take on serious proportions in April this year. There were also indications that the intensity of the threats against *Ilanga* increased when we began to publish fairly serious and critical articles in English, including a series of articles which made dramatic revelations about the Kagiso Trust. We published its full budget; we showed conclusively from Kagiso documents how it was totally politically controlled by one organisation; we showed that people who got bursaries were chosen for their political beliefs. So whatever people may say, and whatever procedures are adopted, the policy is clear. As you know they control very large sums of money. The budget for this year is R119 million.

In conclusion then, I think it is ironical that there were two articles in particular that seem to have not gone down well with those behind the intimidation against us. The first was published on 12 April 1990 and sought to analyse the mass stayaways and the pressure brought to bear on people, and the intimidation used to make these stayaways effective. The heading was 'Coercion or Democracy'. The second dealt at length with the origins of violence and the campaign to isolate Inkatha and its president. The heading read 'Politics by Panga'. Sadly it seems that that has in fact become the ground-rule of politics in South Africa today.

3. WHAT HOPE POLITICAL PLURALISM IN SOUTH AFRICA?

THE NATURE OF BLACK FEARS AND ASPIRATIONS

CONNIE MOLUSI

Journalist at SAPA

Today we are witnessing the ghastly consequences of the culture of violence that has become an integral part of South African society. For a long time we have condoned and nurtured violence in the name of the liberation struggle. That violence hasn't abated. In fact it seems it is going to remain with us for much longer. There is no tolerance of different political viewpoints, and I think the blame doesn't lie simply with one organisation — it spreads across other organisations. I don't think that one single party is to be blamed for it. We are living at a time when social and political violence has become so routinised, so endemic in our townships, that it appears to have evolved into a normal state of affairs. And new areas of violence are opening up.

Sometimes it even seems that the situation was preferable when political organisations were denied the right to organise openly. We obviously note an increase in political violence, particularly after 2 February this year, and it is continuing at an alarming rate. Innocent people are being caught in that crossfire. The leadership of political organisations has made appeals for an end to it. They issue statements condemning brutal acts of violence, but the killing continues unabated. In fact it is becoming increasingly evident that the situation has grown beyond the powers of leaders to address, and I think the culture of resistance politics actually is or was responsible for the present scenario.

To a very large extent I would attribute the current political intolerance to the period popularly known as the mass insurrection era spanning 1984 to 1986, when a culture of people's war was born, which assumed ideological homogeneity among black people; and as a result you had the formation of street committees pursuing the political aims and objectives of particular community organisations. No-one could absent himself from those street committees because he would then be declared an 'enemy of the struggle', therefore you had to participate even if you were opposed to the decisions being made. Street committees are again on the increase in the townships. Ironically they are structured, basically, to discuss the political programmes of a single organisation. However, attendance is compulsory for people living in a particular area.

The type of democracy that has arisen in the process of the liberation struggle has raised serious fears for the future. When the leadership of organisations across the political spectrum continues to condemn violence, and to make prolific speeches and pleas for it to end, it doesn't seem that the message is filtering through to their constituencies or their membership.

You know, some people who are getting caught in this crossfire simply see the current scenario as a foretaste of things to come. In fact things have got so much worse that people have even started to prescribe to other people whether they can go and bury someone they know or someone they have been associated with. Some four or five weeks back, people were actually assaulted for having attended the funeral of a person who was quite respectable politically, was a hated person in government circles, had spent a number of years in prison, and died through a car accident. I have had the privilege of interviewing some of the people who were assaulted and in their view, for them, the choice is clear, 'If this is what freedom is, if this is what liberation is about, then probably we'd better die before it comes.' The harassment of these particular people hasn't abated. Last week one young boy, who was assaulted for attending the funeral, was assaulted again for making press statements and giving interviews to journalists. When his elder brother tried to investigate why this particular funeral should have been out of bounds, he was stabbed and at this moment is lying critically ill in hospital. I think this is a classic illustration of the violent syndrome that for quite some time we have nurtured, and have been afraid to speak about. It has developed into a monster that is threatening the basic fabric of our civilised society.

For some ordinary people there is a very pertinent question that arises. They have supported the liberation struggle to date, they thought it had noble goals, but they are unable to put up with the reality of what they thought was the opening of a new era.

I think that as long as political organisations or liberation movements don't re-examine their culture of mobilisation this scenario is not going to change. In any community there are people of different political persuasions. Sometimes there is a call to isolate an organisation, but you can't expect members of that organisation to participate in the isolation of their own ideals or convictions. That is surely a recipe for a violent response to blatant political intimidation. I think for as long as political organisations continue to fight for political hegemony, to see themselves as sole representatives of black people, the violence is not going to end.

First of all, townships are not made up of people supportive of one organisation only. You would know that whatever political programme you are setting up in your mobilisation campaign, you would have to develop the necessary sensitivity to other people's views. But that doesn't seem to be the practice, nor does it seem that it is going to be the practice in the short term or for the foreseeable future.

In fact on the contrary, for some people the prospect of negotiations only spells gloom. Their hopes of freedom, their hopes of new opportunities, are simply being dashed, and liberation has become anathema to them. I think it is quite true that leaders of political organisations are simply shy of critical debate on their political programmes, debate which is very important for democracy. We seem to have been caught up within the culture that was developed when political activity wasn't free, when liberation organisations developed a democracy with its own definition, and anyway probably most people sympathised with that as they couldn't go into open political activities without incurring the wrath of the state.

However I think things have changed and these changes should also now be applied to methods of mobilisation and political campaigning. Disappointingly this is not happening, and until it does there is no hope for political pluralism. What is left lingering among ordinary people, especially those without very strong political views, is a curse on the era we're living in. The unbanning of political organisations is seen as a curse, because within it new frontiers of violence have opened up; leadership's intervention is failing to bring peace, is failing to bring stability. All that remains is the concern that a future South Africa will simply become another dictatorship, another totalitarian state.

These views, of course, are very hurtful for people like myself to have reached, but I think they arise from a very genuine concern for the victims of the senseless violence of people who don't like to hear a different view from their own, which they have defined as sacrosanct. Anybody who dares choose to differ with them is castigated as a sellout, and has to be deprived of a roof over his head, or hacked to death with pangas.

I think for as long as political organisations cannot develop a sensitivity to their differences, cannot come together to agree on what these are, there is no hope for pluralism. With that particular gloom, all that is left of the aspirations of people who participated in the liberation struggle are fears of worse things to come, and I think those fears are not far-fetched.

Then one question that lingers is, when is this madness going to end? I think the point has to be driven home to the black political organisations that the violence cannot be tolerated for much longer, that they need to sit around and resolve their problems. If that is not going to happen, the future is very bleak and holds no hope for democracy or any prosperity. All that has been said about the aspirations of the people was simply the rhetoric of people competing for political positions, and this democracy wasn't actually the democracy that people, or people who support these organisations, thought they had been advocating. Black fears nowadays have actually by far surpassed aspirations for the future.

It is interesting that for some time people couldn't put on their political T-shirts because they feared the state, but currently putting on an organisation's T-shirt puts you at risk of becoming a panga victim, a tyre victim, or having your house petrol-bombed. I find it interesting that people have resorted to the very tactics they so strenuously criticised when it was the state that used them. For years they had criticised the government about the lack of democracy, and about prohibiting open political activities. They stressed the right to all freedoms, including freedom of the press, freedom of association and freedom of expression. But it has become apparent that they understood little about those particular freedoms. I think that it is the role of every responsible and concerned South African to start thinking about ways and means of saving our townships from developing into another Beirut, saving South Africa from becoming another Mozambique, or just another Angola. And the sooner people stand up courageously to challenge undemocratic political practices the better, otherwise there is no future for this country, this country is doomed.

4. WHITHER BLACK ART? THE CULTURAL DESKS

KAIZER NYATSUMBA

Poet, writer, senior political journalist on The Star

African literature, I believe, really came of age in 1986 when the much coveted literary prize and ultimate honour, the Nobel Prize for Literature, was awarded to one of Africa's talented and richly deserving writers, Nigerian Wole Soyinka. The awarding of this precious literary prize to Soyinka, the first African writer to be thus honoured, did not mark the beginning of African literature, however. What the award did mark, even though very belatedly, was the formal acknowledgement by the book-reading world that literature written by blacks or by Africans was comparable to the best anywhere in the world.

Now important though this acknowledgement was, it certainly didn't go without its share of controversy. Some radical African writers, while congratulating Soyinka on being awarded the Nobel Prize, pointed out that the award constituted a recognition of African literature by the West, and thus perpetuated in their minds the mistaken and offensive belief that the West was not only superior to Africa but was also qualified to pass judgement, such as whether African literature was good enough and deserving of international recognition. There were those, too, who questioned what they called the use of Western standards to judge African literature. They advocated what they called black aesthetics in evaluating African literature and went as far as suggesting that Africa should have its own equivalent of the Nobel Prize in literature. But that, ladies and gentlemen, is not for us to go into in this paper.

What we do want to point out, however, is the fact that attitudes towards African literature suddenly changed, even in some of the most conservative universities around the world. Works by African writers found their way into the curricula of a number of universities' English departments and some universities introduced or strengthened existing African Literature or African Studies departments. Here in South Africa this move has been very slow and painful for those who had grown accustomed to regarding works by blacks as marginal and undeserving of rigorous academic attention.

Internationally renowned though he is, Soyinka has had to endure some spells in prison in his country under the various regimes. His was by no means an exceptional case. As Lewis Nkosi quite correctly points out in a discussion on literature and liberation, some of Africa's leading writers like Kenya's Ngugi wa Thiong'o, Nigeria's Wole Soyinka and Chinua Achebe, Ghana's Kofi Awoonor and Sierra Leone's Yulisa Amadu Maddity, have either endured prison spells in their respective countries or been forced into exile.

In his discussion of the role of the writer in the liberation struggle, Lewis Nkosi says there are at least two stages during which a writer can make a contribution. These stages, Nkosi says, are the actual struggle for liberation, when writers attempt to capture in their pamphlets, poems, novels and plays what he calls 'the revolutionary impulse of which they are inalienably a part'; and secondly the period of reconstruction which follows the successful conclusion of the wars of liberation when, according to Nkosi, 'Writers register not only the pain and joy of national rebirth, but begin to constitute an important source of consciousness for the nation.' The second phase, Nkosi warns, is fraught with risks and dangers and 'inaugurates the most dangerous relationship between the writers and the party in power'.

Achebe and Ngugi immediately come to mind here. Both were popular writers in their countries during the liberation struggle. Indeed, Achebe's eloquent and passionate cry against colonialism in his famous *Things Fall Apart* remains unrivalled in my opinion even today. Strange though it is, these yesterday's heroes have been persecuted by successive post-colonial governments and now live in exile. It is therefore not surprising, I think, that both Ngugi and Achebe have now taken to condemning despotism and dictatorship in their recent writings. Ngugi gave us among other books *Devil on the Cross* a few years ago, and more recently, *Matigari*. These, and Achebe's recent *Anthills of the Savannah*, very eloquently decry dictatorship.

My brief here is to discuss the political role of black writers, poets, actors and musicians, and to take a look at the future through the prophetic eyes of art. Let me say right now that I am not a firm believer in the reduction of art to mere political statements and slogans. If I had had my way I would have chosen for discussion today a topic which would have asserted art's inviolate autonomy and independence from politics. If my opening remarks have not already given my bias away, I will now let it be known that this paper will look critically at the current cultural debate, briefly evaluate the contributions made by the different phases of black South African literature, and speculate on the future of this literature in a post-apartheid South Africa.

The question, I think, which needs to be asked from the very beginning is whether there is any role in the political arena for artists. My answer is a hesitant 'yes' which needs to be qualified. Here, of course, we will have to concede the obvious: firstly, that black writers in this country come from the oppressed community which forms the bottom stratum of South African life. (By blacks, I hasten to add, I refer to Africans, Indians and coloured people.) Needless to say these writers have been at the receiving end of hundreds of laws made in an unrepresentative all-white parliament, specifically aimed at suppressing, oppressing and depriving blacks of anything of consequence. Surely this is a truth which needs no saying, just as it is a truism that these writers' communities have been characterised mostly by abject poverty and deprivation among other things. Insofar as these writers are members of such destitute communities it was therefore to be expected, I think, that most of them would rebel against the status quo and seek to expose its ills and the ravages visited upon them. Works such as Lewis Nkosi's *Mating Birds*, Ingoapele Madingoane's *Africa My Beginning*, and Don Mattera's *Azanian Love Song* have done this admirably in my opinion. While these works inevitably belong to the protest or resistance literature category, at the end of the day they remain works of art capable of proudly standing on their own on literary merit. The same, however, cannot be said about some of the poems and short stories thoughtlessly churned out in the 1970s and even today. And so I am for the kind of writing which is socially aware and uses as its point of departure observations of things happening in and around the writers' communities. The end product must, however, be a work of art and not merely political propaganda or slogans. That is the role I see for artists in the political arena which is already crowded with capable activists, politicians and political propagandists.

Writing on the same issue, namely the role of writers in the struggle, the late Dr Richard Rive was quite emphatic: 'The only difference between the writer and the black man in the ghetto is that the writer is the articulate black man in the ghetto, and he is therefore better able to express himself through words. Otherwise he is indistinguishable from the non-writer and, what is more, is treated no differently by the South African authorities. He reacts in the same way given the same conditions and is as aroused when flogged with quirts or blasted with teargas. Then he retaliates by angrily recording his experiences or throwing stones at casspirs or both. He is not either a literary person or a political activist. Nor can he be forced to perform both functions with equal attention. There will always be a difference of emphasis. His status as a writer can never protect him from being shot at, his poetry can never deflect bullets, but he has one important advantage: he is able to translate his experiences and emotions into words. Often he recalls the happenings in red-hot prose and lurid description, to the despair of academic purists, at other times he paints his strokes with quiet subdued brushwork to the despair of the literary activist overseas.'

Dr Rive is quite serious about one thing, and that is: writers should be allowed to do their work, which is, according to him, 'to define and record', without any interference from either the state or activists. A writer, Dr Rive argues, is 'an articulate memory of his oppressed people'.

Now black South African literature has gone through at least three stages and is presently going through the fourth one. The fifth stage, it seems to me, ought to be well under way by now but sad to say it does not seem to have begun.

The first stage began in the 19th century with the appearance in missionary publications and newspapers of didactic poems with a Christian slant or flavour. It culminated in the publication by the Lovedale Press, still in the 19th century, of Sol T Plaatje's *Mhudi: An Epic of South African Native Life a Hundred Years Ago*, which was the first known novel by a black South African to be published. These works, without fail, tended to be very British in language and style and were meant to instil morals and teach Christianity to blacks.

The second stage began, in my view, with the founding of *Drum* magazine in 1951. The black writers of the day, most of whom were journalists working for *Drum* magazine – Lewis Nkosi, Can Themba and Es'kia Mphahlele, became disaffected with British morals and Christianity, and started experimenting with township lingo in their writings. Though more politically conscious than their immediate predecessors these writers did not directly engage politics and the government of the day in their writings. They were subtle and philosophical in their denunciation of apartheid and some of them, such as Can Themba and Todd Matshikiza, were endowed with a sense of humour, devastating wit and acerbic sarcasm.

The 1960s and 1970s saw the emergence of a new generation of writers who fall in what I call the third stage of black South African literature. Names like Oswald Mbuyiseni Mtshali, Mongane Wally

Serote and Mafika Pascal Gwala, among others, belong here. These were angry poets who directly engaged the system in their writings and made no apology for this stance. This was during the halcyon days of black consciousness and these writers were part of that movement. Their poetry was angry and had a dual message: 'Black is beautiful', which was the rallying call of the day, and 'White man, listen!' Their works, though no longer as relevant today as they were then, revolutionised black South African literature in particular and South African literature in general. For blacks it affirmed their pride, dignity and humanity, and for whites it was a glimpse of black South African township life. Out of the collective guilt, white liberal academics patronised these writers' works even if they sometimes thought it was not poetry as they knew it. The three stages outlined above were all important in the development of South African literature. Each one of them contributed towards making literature of South African blacks what it is today.

A question which needs asking, however, is, where are we now? The situation today, I would argue, is not much different from what it was in the 1970s or the early 1980s. Literature written by black South Africans is still aimed primarily at a white book-reading public which forms the bulk of the reading public in this country. There are still those who believe that art and culture are 'instruments of the struggle' and are therefore not supposed to be an 'independent critical voice about our country', as journalist Ivor Powell put it recently in a report on culture in *The Weekly Mail*. When extracts from a paper on culture by African National Congress legal guru Albie Sachs were published in *The Weekly Mail* a few months ago, these sparked off a healthy debate. In his paper Sachs had casually suggested that the phrase 'culture is an instrument of the struggle' be banished from the vocabulary of political activists who had to be persuaded that artists' independence was to be guaranteed and never to be tampered with. While many writers welcomed the timeous publication of Sachs's paper, there were some discordant voices which were not altogether enthusiastic in their response to the paper's publication.

At the launch of the Mass Democratic Movement's national cultural desk in Johannesburg, Pretoria activist and ANC spokesman Naledi Tsiki, standing in for keynote speaker Albie Sachs who could not make it to the conference, reiterated the bit about culture being an instrument of struggle. Tsiki told delegates to the national cultural congress, 'First and foremost culture is an instrument of the struggle. Culture is the soul of the people and therefore it is very important, a very essential instrument of the struggle, it's a very important and essential aspect of the lives of the people both socially and politically. Without the necessary means to organise ourselves culturally we can find ourselves unable to achieve the goals we have set for ourselves.'

Now, as if that was not bad news enough, Tsiki said cultural workers were not only social leaders but were also arbiters of what was and what wasn't progressive art. While criticism which, according to Tsiki, 'the people in the country are satisfied with', was allowed, if cultural workers felt that criticism 'lowered the standard' then they, the cultural workers, could 'devise means and methods of improving that'. They were, in other words, going to be above criticism, they were going to be creators, critics and censors all in one. In his *Weekly Mail* article, Powell summed up Tsiki's attitude thus: 'In the end, though, there was the old arrogance. Culture belongs to the commissars. Culture is the baby sister of politics, to be guided and chastised or indulged and petted at the whim of its social elders. Certainly there was never any sense that an independent critical voice of culture could be one from which we could learn something about either our country or our humanity. One was left with the same old questions about the cultural desk and its satellite structures, seriously and not merely rhetorically. Which people? What culture?'

Now while the views expressed by Tsiki might seem to be representative of the cultural desk, they are however at variance with views expressed by official spokesmen for the African National Congress. At a mammoth festival-cum-conference on 'Culture in another South Africa' held in Amsterdam, Holland, in December 1987, and attended by exiled South African 'cultural workers' as they had themselves called, and many others from within the country, ANC national executive committee member Pallo Jordan said artists' independence was to be respected. Jordan concluded his paper at the conference with this statement: 'In conclusion permit me to address a special word to the family of South African artists and cultural workers; both those in the frontline trenches of the struggle at home, and those who have been forced into exile to pursue their craft. The ANC does not ask you to become political pamphleteers. There are a number of those. Though we need more, the ANC does not require poets to become political sloganeers: the walls of South Africa's cities testify to our wealth in those and the mastery they have of their craft. While we require propaganda we do not demand that every graphic artist and sculptor become a pop artist. We would urge our artists to pursue excellence in their respective disciplines, to be excellent artists and to serve the struggle for liberation with excellent art. But let us remember also that the future imposes grave obligations on us all, artists and non-artists alike.'

Here, in short, is where we are with black South African literature today — in the fourth stage of South African literature's development. It is also a stage characterised by the proliferation of mediocre, so-called committed poetry which denounces the government of the day and its racial policies and extols non-racialism. Also characteristic of this stage is the now pervasive reluctance of publishers to publish poetry and fiction. This contrasts sharply with the situation in the 1970s when anything written by blacks, whether good or bad, was published without any questions. Today, however, publishers concentrate on more lucrative genres such as biographies and autobiographies of accomplished well-known people (mostly activists), children's literature and labour material, to mention a few.

The fifth and final stage I referred to earlier on, a stage which I said should be well under way now, is one in which South African writers will cease to be conditioned by apartheid and its attendant ills but emerge instead simply as writers whose works will have universal appeal and relevance. It is a stage, if you will, in which South African writers of all races will write about South Africans as people and not merely as victims and monsters.

Black South Africans who have hitherto been portrayed as helpless victims of a system which has been decried the world over will have to be portrayed as human beings capable of myriad feelings such as love, hatred, fear, happiness etc. Now I for one, as a black person, am tired of being forever portrayed as a victim in works of art, and would like to be presented as an all-round human being for a change.

For far too long now South African art, ranging from literature and drama through to music, has thrived on apartheid for its recognition and relevance. In the music industry South African musicians seem to have benefited from the country's cultural boycott which made it impossible for celebrated overseas musicians to perform in this country; and so the late 1970s and the 1980s have seen the mushrooming of new musicians every day who are never hesitant to embarrass real musicians with their antics and sometimes totally meaningless performances. Whenever one watches TV2 and TV3 there is likely to be a new group that one hasn't seen or heard of before, really doing what people in the townships aptly call 'bubblegum music'. These people and their managers are unabashedly in music to make a quick buck and not to entertain and in the process improve the quality of local music.

For those who advocate the reduction of art into an instrument of the struggle, Professor Es'kia Mphahlele's comments should come in very handy: 'Finally, it is an exaggerated claim for literature that it can spark a revolution. There are surely more immediate irks that incite a revolution, all those irks that arise from a sense of deprivation and loss. People expect to be incited by the language of everyday usage, not the height and form of expression and metaphor of the kind that make imaginative literature. By the time a writer has done composing a play, a poem, a story as a vehicle of political agitation the revolution is on the way. Literature may record, replay, inspire an ongoing process as an act of language that renews and revitalises. It is a vehicle of thought and feeling and should be increased by reliving experiences. Literature is forever stirring us up. This is its own kind of revolution.'

Now black South African artists despite all that has been said above about them do have a few achievements to be proud of. Some of the country's black writers such as Don Mattera, Gcina Mhlope, Miriam Tlali and others are respected abroad as writers and have been honoured in different ways. Short story writer Professor Njabulo Ndebele, now an English professor at the National University of Lesotho, was voted winner of the prestigious Noma Award by Publishing in Africa for his first short story collection, *Fools and Other Stories*. South African playwrights Mbongeni Ngema, Percy Mtwa, Gcina Mhlope and Maishe Maponya, among others, are well known and respected abroad as well. Awards after awards have been given to them in recognition of their talents.

As for good South African musicians, the world is currently opening up for them, thanks to a large extent to American musician Paul Simon. Since the Graceland tour involving Simon and some South African musicians such as Ray Phiri's Stimela and Joseph Tshabalala's Ladysmith Black Mambazo, which later went on to win a Grammy award, a number of local musicians have travelled widely abroad taking their music to parts of the world which, a mere few years ago, had never heard of them. Some of these musicians — and here one thinks specifically of people like Lucky Dube, Johnny Clegg and his Savuka, Simon 'Mahlatini' Nkabinde, and the young Ricardo — have become household names in countries such as the United States, Britain, Jamaica, France and Japan.

So what does the future hold for South African artists? We will start with writers.

My personal view is that unless South African writers radically change direction and outgrow their obsession with apartheid as the content of their writings, their works face the risk of being forgotten in future. Most of the present writings are about the present and they almost always harp on the same thing. Obviously some denounce apartheid in a much better manner artistically than others, but the overwhelming majority of them have been preoccupied in their works with the system and not with human beings and human relations, which is really what makes a good story at the end of the day. Works that will be prescribed in our universities and our schools, then, will tend to be those by South African writers who are presently in exile, as well as those by African writers from the other African countries. Already there is indication that works prescribed in the African literature departments at our universities at undergraduate level are mostly those written by Nigerians, Kenyans and other Africans, not black South Africans.

With the change in the political situation in the country, those black South African playwrights who have capitalised on apartheid for their plays are not likely to find a ready audience for their works abroad any more, and consequently the West will cease to be generous with their awards simply to make a statement against apartheid and express solidarity with the victims of the system.

Black South African musicians who are not opportunists, I think, will continue to find a ready market for their music abroad. It seems to me the mere sound of South African music, be it reggae, soul or mbaqanga, is popular overseas and is likely to continue to be popular. Those musicians, however, who are political opportunists and now want to sing about 'Black President', which happens to be the title of Brenda Fassie's latest album, and sing about politics all of a sudden, when they were never political at any stage, will probably not get as good a reception overseas. It is South African music, mostly black South African music, that people in Asia, Europe, Africa and the Americas want to hear, and not South African politics which they are already tired of, except for die-hard anti-apartheid activists who will not let go of any opportunity to demonstrate their solidarity with the victims of apartheid.

Now that is how I see the arts faring in the country in future. My comments, I hasten to add, are based largely on observations as a journalist and a consumer of art and as a student of literature. That, ladies and gentlemen, is all I have.

5. CENSORSHIP

DAWN LINDBERG

Theatre producer and entertainer

Censorship in any form and from whatsoever direction is dangerous and destructive to the expression of ideas and ideals. No strangers to censorship, Des [Lindberg] and I have been in show business for 25 years, and for 25 years we have been handcuffed by restraints and restrictions and bannings imposed by censors under whatever name they were operating at the time. So to point to the future and to understand what is happening now with our new censorship, I would like to tell you a little bit about the last 25 years of censorship as we have experienced it.

In 1966 our album *Folk on Trek* was banned on the grounds of blasphemy because of its irreverent assertion that 'these bones are going to rise again', and there were one or two risqué nursery rhymes as well. We went to the Supreme Court, the only avenue open to us at the time, and lost the case. All the records were destroyed and South Africa was presumably saved from some unmentionable plague.

In 1973 our production of *Godspell* was also banned outright, again on the grounds of blasphemy. The fact that it was the first public 'no smoke-screen' production in South Africa with a multi-racial cast seemed only to harden the censors' resolve. We won that case after Advocate Anton Mostert persuaded Judge Lammie Snyman to allow one performance at Wits Great Hall at which he might exercise a judgement. He ruled that the play was not blasphemous but that we should preface each performance with the statement, 'What you are about to see is a play!' This was a serious decree. We conjectured it was to make sure that nobody in the audience thought that the crucifixion was real eight times a week.

Our next production, *The Black Mikado*, premiered at the Diepkloof Hall in Soweto in May 1976, not a very peaceful time to be schlepping actors and luring critics into the murky unknown of Soweto, into a hall which was damaged in the unrest two weeks later. We immediately received a letter from Dr Treurnicht, at that time a government minister, saying 'If you do not desist from what you are doing, we have ways and means of making you stop.' I have that letter on file. Tyres were slashed and death threats were received. The SABC subtly shelved our proposals and red-pencilled our songs.

Racial segregation was of course the most insidious censorship of all, since it meant control of who should reveal what to whom in the theatre. In July 1977 the South African Association of Theatre Managements made urgent representations to the government, and in August of the same year all theatres in South Africa were finally allowed to open their doors to all races, so I'd just like to point out that in fact the theatres were the very first bastions of apartheid to go, long before sport, restaurants or hotels.

The Best Little Whorehouse in Texas was our next production. We now knew to budget costs of likely litigation. This time the title was banned. Advocate Jules Browde won this case before the newly constituted Publications Control Board on the grounds of possible confusion with the popular family television series *Little House on the Prairie* if the word 'whore' was tastefully omitted from the title. So we got our title back. Ladies and gentlemen, you certainly have to retain your sense of humour if you want to survive in this business.

In the past five years the censorship system matured somewhat, and under the enlightened restraint of Professor Kobus van Rooyen, who recently retired, more movies were shown unscathed and plays allowed to be staged — pubic hair, four-letter words and all! In fact, we have reason to believe that it is policy to let the liberal fringe lefties indulge their needs and sublimate freely within the safe precincts of the alternative theatre venues.

Ironically, after all these years of the iron-clad, all pervading government fist, focus has now turned instead to the new problems facing the South African theatre and film performance, and entertainment: the hardening in attitudes of the authors of the cultural boycott, and the new censorship body, the cultural desk of the left.

When working on *King Africa* for PACT [the Performing Arts Council of the Transvaal] in 1988 we discovered, with some dismay, that we were now under pressure and virtually obliged and coerced to submit the script for assessment by a desk who would judge its relevance to the struggle before giving the green light to actors to audition and perform, or for audiences to attend. The theme of *King Africa* was the importance of education for all, and that the pen is mightier than the sword, a similar theme to Fugard's *My Children! My Africa!* An even bigger problem, however, was that we were working for PACT, an organisation which receives state subsidies, even although we explained that (a) PACT was nonracial and (b) their only involvement in *King Africa* was that they picked up all costs including salaries for two hundred black actors, singers, technicians and stage hands.

Meanwhile, unconnected with *King Africa*, we had rights to another musical from the States, *Your Arm's Too Short to Box with God*, which were summarily taken away in terms of the cultural boycott because we were white producers. We met with Archbishop Tutu who prayed with us and shook his head, saying that there was no such thing as conditional sanctions. There are other works where the authors state categorically that it is simply not worth the international pressure to risk giving rights to South Africans at present, even in spite of our track record and that of many of our other producers.

With the cultural boycott against South Africa, Broadway and West End works were denied us, but focus then turned to the creation of indigenous theatre, and this was of course good in a lot of ways. There is much creativity going on that is vital and daring, innovative, and starting from a truly African-based culture, but unfortunately there is a downside: without the stimulation from a broader selection of work from other parts of the world, we are in danger of becoming insular and narrowly blinkered. There is also too much formula protest theatre which is didactic and polemic, instead of portraying three-dimensional characters or real-life situations. Could it be that if you rail loudly enough and lecture long enough there may be a ticket waiting to fame and fortune in faraway lands? It is a trap for writers and producers to avoid.

Mbongeni Ngema's vibrant, energetic and highly entertaining work *Township Fever* was doing extremely good business here and obviously designed for world travel, but he underwent a lot of protest from the unions and the cultural desk, and actually agreed to change sections of his script, so that it would more clearly support the struggle. I think that is iniquitous.

I have always stood for an open society where people in all their chosen careers are given equal opportunities to rise to the top, and everyone is judged purely on merit and performance. I also feel strongly that all doors for discussion and exchange of ideas must at all times be open. How can we begin to solve our problems in this tormented and beloved country of ours if we are always blinkered and restricted and silenced and cut off from one another and instructed on whose platform we may write and perform? After all, to know what is going on in the streets and in the minds of people is very helpful in seeking remedies and solutions and answers.

There is only one essential factor that sets man apart from the rest of the animal species, and that is the power of reason. Are our governments both in Pretoria and in exile too afraid to allow a free flow of reasonable thought? Censorship is indeed dictatorship of the mind. Let the people decide!

In recent months a few new ripples of hope have emerged. Firstly, there are signs that the cultural boycott will be the first to lift, as it is lifting already. We hope that it will lift freely, however, and not in terms of behind-the-doors exchanges of favours or assurances that a certain platform or a certain polemic will be adhered to. However, as the theatre was the first to open its doors to all races, in 1977, so the cultural boycott, it seems to me, will be the first of the sanctions to lift, and I think this will have extremely positive results, in terms of the inflow of vital, new and fresh ideas.

The cultural desk itself is, I think, aware of the dangers of censorship of the mind and in particular of cultural thought, and they are trying very hard, or certainly making a sincere effort, to move away from the kind of dictatorship and censorship that we have had to endure over the last forty years. Let us hope that they have learned their lessons, from the powers that be, who are fast crumbling.

6. TIME TO SPEAK OUT

LIONEL ABRAHAMS

Writer, poet, publisher

A writer and activist I know has remarked that our historical moment may prove to have enjoyed more freedom of expression than either the apartheid past or the barely foreseeable future. If we want to establish habits of liberty, the time to scrutinise the candidates for power, define individual rights, check the ideological abuse of language, and speak out, is now.

The type of dangers that demand our vigilance can be indicated by the idiosyncratic employment of two words. 'Democratic' is overemployed, most frequently to denote 'approved by a self-styled democratic committee of some sort'. Increasingly, the pristine connection between 'democracy' and the expression of individual choices is attenuated. Certainly, the second half of the democratic contract is the agreement to bow to the will of the majority. But in our day 'democratic' applies increasingly to decisions emerging from political machines, and all too often individual ideas and desires are over-ridden with no reference at all to popular preference. It is a telling circumstance that one political conglomerate chose to call itself the Mass Democratic Movement, as though 'democracy' admitted the possibility of an Elite Democratic Movement!

'Censorship', on the other hand, has had its sense both expanded and contracted, and that by one and the same body, the Anti-Censorship Action Group. ACAG's monthly bulletin, *Update,* lists as instances of 'censorship' a surprising range of phenomena: magisterial refusals of permission to hold protest marches, certain indictments and imprisonments — any (preferably official) behaviour, in fact, that can be construed as infringing freedom of expression. On the other hand, *Update* maintains a silence over the ANC's selective cultural boycott.

As I see it, a selective proscription of cultural exchanges — even more than a blanket boycott on commerce with a pariah country — perfectly expresses the spirit of censorship: 'Thou shalt express nothing that offendeth me nor anything that comforteth mine enemy.' As a still disenfranchised party, the ANC does not yet command governmental powers with which to enforce its proscriptions; the best it can do is operate certain machinery – such as the lapsed and discredited 'cultural desk' – to obstruct cultural acts it disapproves of. But the ANC aspires to hegemony over us all and (despite the liberal acknowledgement, by an engaging apologist like Albie Sachs, that artistic pursuits must take the politically recalcitrant ways of individuality, subtlety, variety and unpredictability) shows no sign of a perception that an instrument like the selective cultural boycott is inimical to the pluralistic spirit of genuine democracy.

7. THE SOWETO SCHOOLS

NOMAVENDA MATHIANE

Author and assistant editor of Frontline

I want to talk on the quiet and slow collapse of Soweto schools. I am going to talk about the how and not the why. I will leave the why to the politicians and academics. I am also going to talk about how politics has influenced education. As I stand here I am wearing a number of caps. I am a mother, I am a journalist, and I am a community worker. I have three children, aged 24, 20 and 18. I am telling you their ages not because I want you to guess my age — you will never guess that — but so that you may know that the matter is very close to my heart, because all three of my children have been affected by the collapse.

The eldest tried to write matric for five years. Ultimately I took her to Lesotho where she did her O-levels and is now battling with A-levels. My boy of 20 got stuck at matric last year like many other youths in Soweto. One afternoon my youngest, then 14, came back home and said boys were brandishing guns at school, and I realised that one day I would get a call to say that my daughter was dead, a casualty of the struggle. So I just had to take her out of the black school situation.

I've decided I'm going to talk about the period 1984 to 1986, then move over to 1986 to 1989, and then deal with 1990. When in 1984 Lekoa [Sebokeng, Sharpeville and other townships in the Vaal Triangle] went up in flames, inevitably Soweto was roped in, and many other black townships. But at the time in Soweto there were already a number of particular problems. There was the Warara Zim-zim* war where children were killing each other in the classrooms, where there was fighting in the streets everywhere. There were strikes within the schools: demands were being made that the DET [Department of Education and Training] allow SRCs [Students' Representative Councils]

---

* Warara: from Afrikaans: waar-waar? (where-where?) meaning they don't know where they are, they are wishy-washy (applied to Comrades by rival groups).

Zim-zim: militant youth wing of AZASM (Azanian Students' Movement) (pronounced Aza-zim); the name also contains a reminder of -zimu, -zimuzimu (Zulu): cannibal.

to operate in black schools; children wanted the scrapping of age limits; and quite a number of other things. So there was confrontation between the students and the DET. At this stage there wasn't any real schooling. In the morning children would go to school and by eleven o'clock they were sauntering back home, you know they were being told not to go to school, not to write examinations and what have you. At that time a number of community workers were very concerned, we were saying, 'What can we do as parents? What can we do as educated people? How can we put our heads together?'

One day in 1986 (I was working, I was doing my stories), I stumbled into a house in Diepkloof where people were talking about the crisis. One woman was very vocal about it, and said, 'We need as black people to stand up and do something about the situation. Let's meet, let's call a meeting of Soweto parents and get our children to go back to school.' A meeting was held in Soweto and the Soweto Education Crisis Committee was born. Later, a meeting to thrash out national educational matters was held in Durban, where the NECC [National Education Crisis Committee] was formed.

At this stage political posturing was already taking place. Even people who had their hearts in the right place, and who wanted education in Soweto to go on, or academics very keen on doing something, soon saw that NECC had been hijacked by the political activists. Within a very short time it was no longer a community organisation, but a UDF-aligned organisation, and therefore most of the academics pulled out, and many others who were not academics. But we live in a country where if you ask questions you are branded an apologist for apartheid, and people just said, well, if that's the route NECC has decided to take, let's disassociate ourselves from it.

In the meantime the situation was going from bad to worse. What was happening in the schools was terrible. Girls were being raped in the classrooms and those boys were not taken to court — it wasn't seen as a criminal offence. Teachers' car tyres were being slashed. Principals' cars were being set alight and the culprits were not brought to book, because if you decided to go and lay a charge you were seen as a bad element and might be necklaced or have your house gutted.

All these things were dividing the children and the community even more, and people kept on saying politicians must keep out of the schools.

So each year the children would go to school in January, and maybe attend school in February as well. In March there would be a boycott, from March to October there would be continuous boycotting, with calls for all sorts of demands to be met. In November the children would either refuse to write and want a postponement of examinations, or they would go to the exam classrooms with papers that had been leaked. Come the end of the year, they had failed.

The NECC, on the other hand, was banned. There was also talk of 'people's education', and each time we asked, 'What's this people's education, is it a curriculum, is it a syllabus, is it a subject?' we got no answer. 'No no no, it's not that,' we were told, 'but we'll come up with a document to tell you what it is.'

All these things confused the people more and more. Some parents took their children out of the black schools and sent them to private schools, or to the homelands. The ordinary person, who could not afford the private schools or to send their child to the homelands, was stuck with the schools in Soweto. Each year at the beginning of January we would meet to discuss the same problems.

What was interesting about the 1990 meeting was this: people had already taken positions. There is this particular group that has to be seen all the time to be in the forefront of everything. When we assembled at Funda Centre as concerned parents, I saw very few concerned parents from the lower working class, but I saw many educated people whose children were in private schools. I saw many political activists, and many teachers who were not prepared to talk, and to me that raised a question mark. What raised another one was the sight of a flag of the ANC, and immediately I knew that we were in for trouble, because here we were, ordinary people gathered to try and deal with a problem, but here was an ANC flag, and within the meeting I could see BC [Black Consciousness] elements, ANC elements and ordinary people. The media were there in full force, and I also knew that overseas viewers and readers would assume, from the presence of the flag, that this very big crowd was mustered entirely by the ANC.

By the end of the day we were as divided as the shades of our colour. Some people were saying we should adopt a resolution that the children go back to school, others that those present should confirm their allegiance to a document supporting the NECC. Many refused, because they knew NECC was aligned to the UDF and some of us were not UDF. Some people said, 'We have really wasted our time. We have not come here to solve our problems, we have come here on a ticket that we did not know. We were supposed to tackle the schooling crisis and we didn't, we wasted a whole day!' The meeting ended in such disarray that we left without singing *Nkosi Sikelel' iAfrika*.

So there we were again with, 'What do we do as parents?' At that very time NEUSA [the National Education Union of South Africa] came on the scene, and some of us were quite excited, here was a fresh group of teachers who might breathe new ideas into the teaching fraternity; but it wasn't long before we were told that NEUSA was also affiliated to the UDF. Teachers who were not interested in being UDF-affiliated were now being forced to join NEUSA, and they were objecting and saying, as teachers who may be aligned to BC or PAC, why don't we have our own union to cater for our needs, as NACTU [the National Congress of Trade Unions] represents many who do not adhere to COSATU [the Congress of South African Trade Unions]. A third group felt the profession was well served by the non-aligned TUATA [the Transvaal United African Teachers' Association]. So we had that rending within the teaching fraternity.

Now in our schools there is the old guard, the old teacher whose primary interest is the child. He is being torn apart by the young teacher who may have been a 1976 student and have an unfinished agenda. At this point in black schools you have divisions: within one school the old teachers are being harassed by the young teachers who are using young militant students. These may not be members of the school, they may be students from other schools, or they may not even be students, but old children of about 25 years who will never get matric anyway, and who should be somewhere else. These are the activists who will harass the old teachers and say, 'You are not going to go to school — you must stay home because you do not want to tackle the DET.'

So come 1990, NEUSA is whipping up people's emotions and teachers don't know what to do. They decide that they are going to march to Braamfontein to the DET office. Then the events in the country overtake them. On 11 February, Mr Mandela comes out, it was a Sunday. On Monday the children don't go to school, they wait for him at Orlando Stadium. On Tuesday they wait for him at FNB [First National Bank] Stadium, and he addresses them and says, 'Students go back to school.' No sooner does he sit down, than one of the UDF members picks up the mike and says, 'Teachers, go to the march tomorrow.' From that day on, that's February, high school children (the primary schools are more or less normal) have been in and out of school, they have held marches, they have just not been schooling, especially in Soweto schools.

My brief here is to say that for as long as the schools are controlled by politicians, the politicians are going to mess up the education of the black child, and I cannot see a black child taking over without education. So until the politicians leave the academics to get on with the business of educating the black children we are in for a very hard time.

8. THE CHILD MASTERS

JOE THLOLOE

Assistant editor, Sowetan

The violence in the townships today is not the most important problem facing this country. The blood-letting is going to come to an end; we are going to be shocked by the amount of blood we have lost; and we will go back to our homes and come to our senses.

The most important problem facing us is education. Let me put my talk backwards; let me start with the solutions. I think we need to restore the confidence of the teachers. We need to give teachers a sense of leadership in the community, that sense they no longer have. I think at the political level we need inspired leadership, leadership that can inspire action. Very sadly the leadership we have today is not that leadership. I believe we need to pool our resources, massive resources, money, men, everything. Finally, I believe the long-term solution is to restructure the system of education.

It is a question of culture. Since 1976 we have developed a new culture. Kids went into the street with petrol bombs and they felt power, and we have never been able to stop that. What has happened since 1976 is that two cultures are developing in the townships. There are the elites who because of the breakdown in black education have been able to get admittance to white schools. There are those who have been able to get to the better schools, private schools. That is one culture that is developing, an elitist culture. But the kid in the township no longer has any motivation to do anything except wield his bottle of petrol.

It has become obvious that DET's education will not work. I thought we were aware of that ages ago — it is not something new. One of my major accusations against white South Africa is that they saw black education deteriorating and did nothing about it. Every businessman here knows the quality of the applications he gets from people with matriculation, from people with degrees, people who are supposed to be fully qualified. There have always been two responses. The one is, 'Let's give him a chance; we need a black face in our company.' The other has been, 'He is not good enough; we can't accept him in our

51

company.' But nobody has ever said 'Let's do something about black education.' Through the years, I know, there have been token donations to black schools in Soweto. A blackboard here, a couple of books there, a bursary to one or two brilliant students, but in the end there has been no concerted voice saying, 'We need to do something about black education.'

Everybody took white superiority for granted. Everybody. Today when we are looking at the future of the country we are all guilty. We, the parents in the townships, for having allowed our kids to go out there with the petrol bombs. They have intimidated us. We ourselves are not saying or doing anything. Today SAYCO [the South African Youth Congress] is saying no black person is to come to work on Monday. It is not the parents out there taking the decisions, it's the little boys, little girls. We are guilty. We are guilty of not having fought bantu education, we the black parents. We left it to the kids of 1976 to say 'Down with bantu education!'

But again we are guilty at another level. We sent two messages to our children. We said to them bantu education is bad, it is poison. That has been a song that we have been singing since 1953. But at the same time we were taking our children to go and drink of that poison, so the kids are confused. They do not understand a person saying, 'Go to school,' and at the same time saying, 'Bantu education is poison.'

I suggest three solutions:

One, a method must be found of giving the black teacher back his confidence. You don't do that by dragging him into organisations like NEUSA [the National Education Union of South Africa] where he in fact joins the schoolboys without any clear sense of direction. They tell him when to go to the DET offices to protest. They tell him when to come into the classroom, and he is then a 'progressive' teacher. We need to pool our minds, bring them together and find a way of restoring the authority of the teacher.

And two, we must restore the authority of the parent.

Both of these can come once we have a very strong leadership that says, 'This is the direction we are taking.' The leadership we have at the moment vacillates. One day it is saying every child must go back to school. The next day it concedes to the demands of the children not to go to school, and it clouds things in very ambivalent language.

We have seen examples of leadership that can inspire confidence among the kids. Pace College in Soweto, where kids still go to school in their uniform, still report to school at the right hour and knock off at the right hour, is an island in this whole madness of Soweto. Somehow a person has got there who can inspire confidence, who can give directions.

Thirdly, by pooling our resources we need to revamp the system. We can't today be arguing about this, it's so obvious that if you are going to give a white child five times what you give a black child for his education, black education is going to be bad and is going to deteriorate as the white education improves.

I am trying to throw a challenge to everybody, that we are responsible, we need to be doing something about our education.

9. DISCUSSION

After the papers had been presented, questions were invited from the audience:

What projects have journalists tried to come up with to create a culture of tolerance and persuade the community of the necessity of basic freedoms?

Thami Mazwai cited the *Sowetan*'s 'nation-building' campaign as such a project.

It was launched in 1988 in a historic speech by the editor, Mr Aggrey Klaaste, and continued since then in the columns of the newspaper. It aimed at involving all political schools of thought in an attempt to rebuild community structures, develop businesses and find a way to get the schools to function properly.

The campaign had been heavily criticised, however, in some quarters. Mr Klaaste was called to a meeting of a particular organisation and asked why he didn't make 'nation-building' part of their campaign. He said he didn't want it to follow any specific political philosophy because other political groups would not participate in it, and he wanted everybody to be involved. Spokesmen of the organisation in question said that for that reason they could not touch it.

Mr Mazwai said it was difficult for the media to come up with anything, because people had taken positions and could not deviate from them for fear of getting into trouble with the young comrades, or being seen by their neighbours as carriers of some sort of disease.

There could be no political pluralism without a systematic grassroots campaign from the political organisations themselves, to try and educate their people about the meaning of the various freedoms, and teach them the guiding principle: 'If at all I differ with you, you must accept that I have a right to differ with you. I am not necessarily against you because I differ with you.'

Connie Molusi said, 'The question exposes our inadequacies,' and explained that journalists could hardly lead campaigns for tolerance. He stressed that it was not one particular political organisation that harassed journalists, but that 'they all do it'.

'You go to a rally, you make your assessment of what the numbers of people are, you try to confirm that with colleagues around you, you get the number.' He said the organisation that held the rally then

55

accused you of underestimating the attendance, and if you raised the matter with certain organisations, you were running risks.

He mentioned a common experience of journalists requesting interviews: 'As soon as you say who you are, the name of the newspaper which you represent, suddenly a person is not around, he is at endless meetings, he is not available.'

How representative are you of feelings in journalist circles?

Mr Mazwai replied, 'Let me not be accused of racism. I think that black journalists are by and large trying to be very objective. Some of them may not be doing it willingly, but they are being forced by circumstances.'

Explaining this, he said there was a widespread perception that charterist groups had far more control than others in the townships — partly because the ANC and the UDF had an organisational structure superior to that of AZAPO. But in specific areas Africanists and black consciousness groups were extremely strong, and the PAC and AZAPO groups could not be ignored. Black journalists coming from that sort of background knew how dangerous it was to operate from this direction, and as a result they were forced to be very objective.

Black journalists knew, he said, that emotions in the black community, or any other, could be influenced, and opinions swayed. 'A strong campaign will produce a lot of support for say, the ANC, and then the PAC will come up with a campaign and that whole mass of people will support that campaign. Then the BCM [Black Consciousness Movement] will campaign, and those same people who were singing ANC slogans will be backing the BCM, because basically the ordinary man in the street, all he wants is liberation, and he's not very choosy about where that liberation comes from.'

On the other hand, many white journalists, even some white editors, had decided that one particular organisation was the best for this country. 'Being a journalist, I know that a lot of us believe we are God's gift to mankind,' he said. 'White journalists see it as their duty to try and educate their white readers and show them which is the organisation that must rule them tomorrow. They bend over backwards to ensure that the message goes through, distorting, manipulating facts, ignoring what is happening in the black community.'

Arthur Konigkramer added that for a long time the English-language press, specifically the Argus company, had been very active in opposition, keeping the values of protest and democracy alive. But about 10 or 15 years ago there was a major change: gradually more and more of the senior committed journalists moved away from newspapers, so that these were being run more and more by people without much experience. At a more junior level, large numbers of ideologically committed people stayed the course, and these were the advocacy journalists. Mr Konigkramer felt that the press should ensure salaries that would attract and hold journalists of real ability.

Concerning training, he said that in Natal the journalism schools were run by people with a very committed ideological stance, and that journalists from those schools were all in the key positions, writing 'the sensitive news that actually influences people's perceptions'.

Mr Konigkramer then raised what he considered the most critical point. In Natal, for example, 'money from overseas has been used to set up an incredibly efficient network to disseminate information with a chosen perspective. If there is an incident anywhere in the townships, whether planned or totally spontaneous, activists at the scene will gather at a central point in Durban within the hour. A team of four or five "experts" will then be alerted and, having listened to the reports from the activists, will decide on how the incident is to be presented.'

'Selected journalists will then be telephoned, and that is why remarkably similar reports containing words like "violence in the green hills of Inanda" will surface in afternoon newspapers, in morning newspapers and even in overseas newspapers. There are very clever people who have actually decided how this incident is going to be presented. They feed it into the "network" and it comes up not only in the individual newspapers but in the wire services. You get a very manipulative form of news input, and that, in the end, is what influences the general public's perception of what actually happened.'

Does Ilanga criticise Inkatha?

Mr Konigkramer: *'Ilanga* actually publishes a large number of articles that are critical of Inkatha. In fact, we have to walk a tightrope sometimes, because we get extreme pressure also from Inkatha, where at times people lower down accuse us of being agents of the ANC.'

Who is responsible for violence and who not? It seems you can't apportion blame. Journalists should teach tolerance.

Kaizer Nyatsumba pointed out that traditionally, black journalists had seen themselves as people with a cause, anti-apartheid journalists who did not have to choose between black political organisations. But since the emergence of the UDF in 1983, political and ideological lines had been drawn and well defined, and one could easily identify journalists' political allegiances or sympathies by the kind of stories they covered.

So far, he added, Nomavenda Mathiane had been the only courageous journalist: she had criticised all. Others should do the same. It was time to start being critical even-handedly.

Censorship from the left, Mr Nyatsumba said, took a worse form than that from government. When the government detained or arrested a journalist, that journalist suddenly became a hero in the people's eyes, but that was not the case when organisations on the left took action against a journalist. Nobody knew about it. The government was overt, but nobody knew who the censors on the left were. They were very many and very dangerous.

Mr Nyatsumba said he had been manhandled by Inkatha supporters demonstrating against [Archbishop] Tutu on his arrival at Jan Smuts airport in 1988 from one of his many pro-sanctions trips abroad, and for the first time in his life he had been happy to see policemen coming towards him. He had received death threats from the PAC for his critical coverage of a PAC draft economic policy document, which he had reported on accurately, but was accused of fabricating. However, the document had since been published as a book, and widely circulated. He had also been threatened by some elements in the ANC, and in AZAPO. 'No single group on the left is innocent,' he said.

South Africa was heading for typical African press freedom. What was happening on the ground was very far from the multi-party ideal. It was frightening. If the situation did not change there was reason to fear that in the new South Africa the press would be controlled and journalists would be thrown in jail for daring to criticise the government of the day. When leaders of these organisations became cabinet ministers they would not suddenly be tolerant democrats.

Mr Nyatsumba remarked that editorials in certain white newspapers were known for their hardline attitude against the government – they didn't mince their words. Now, however, it was dangerous to be outspoken when it came to the ANC. Many whites who embraced the ANC as the future government were trying to be in its good books. The only attacks on the ANC were roundabout.

White liberals, he said, were guilty of this – they would not attack anything ANC-aligned, for fear of having their liberal credentials questioned. It was the same with many black intellectuals who were silence-beholden. One person he admired was Eugene Nyati, director of the Johannesburg-based Centre for Political Studies, who was vigorously questioning and equally critical of all organisations.

The culture of intolerance was engendered in the black community at the height of the 1984/86 unrest in the townships. Everyone had to be seen to be acting together, so dissenting views were not encouraged. People could not differ publicly even now, without exposing themselves to all kinds of dangers.

In conclusion, Mr Nyatsumba felt black journalists could do a lot. They hadn't done enough. They could and should become much more questioning, much more critical. They could call Mandela, Mothopeng, Mosala to account. They could arrange debates. He did not think they were doing that.

One of the speakers commented that a selective boycott sounded more civilised than the old, crude, blanket boycott, but that it was in fact pernicious. It became not a mere barrier blocking the flow of culture, but a form of prescriptive censorship, a political instrument to decide what should and what should not be permitted:

> 'We need to spell out clearly that we are against censorship. Any freedom for which politics may be striving includes at a very essential place the facilitating of a contact between people's experience and their power of expression. For this reason free literature, free art can become the most powerful kind of political art.'

Mr Nyatsumba said it was important, on principle, to be forthright in one's criticism of structures such as the cultural desk, and not try to sugar-coat that criticism — which was surely the tendency — for fear of seeming to be on the other side. In his view the cultural desk was far from reforming, it was in fact the exact opposite. It believed it had the power to decide for the people what the people would see, by whom they would see it performed, that kind of thing. It was frightening. Indeed, what had been mentioned about Mbongeni Ngema boded very ill for the country. The cultural desk had all the powers. It was not becoming as broadly representative as Dawn Lindberg had implied. It was a UDF creation that had become a Mass Democratic Movement structure and was now a Mass Democratic Movement/ANC structure.

He described how *Tribute* magazine had asked him to write a piece on the South African Musicians' Alliance. Some of the musicians he interviewed had a number of uncomplimentary things to say about the desk. He put these musicians' allegations to the desk, and wrote the story. 'I was called to a meeting. They threatened to boycott *Tribute* magazine because the story had appeared there. No, this dictatorship continues.'

When leaders of different organisations make public announcements that they don't like violence, I want to believe that they really don't want to see people die as they are dying like flies today. Why is it that message cannot penetrate to the grassroots?

Mr Molusi said it was very difficult to control the youth, and they had 'unbelievable power'. Also, leaders tended to deny that their members were responsible for violence, claiming that 'it was only hooligans'. He said political education needed to be taken to the ground where the violence was happening. 'Without that there's no hope.'

Mr Mazwai said, 'Welcome to the club, Kaizer, re harassment. In the past, the leadership was in jail and the youth had a field-day. The present leaders don't have control. As long as they're not threatened they will allow things to go along. It's a power game, and youths are going to do things that please their organisers. Their attitude is, I know necklacing is bad, but if my leader doesn't say anything, I'll go along and do more.'

Mr Mazwai said the convoluted theories of intellectuals had contributed to this. 'For example, a psychology student at university will hear theories about why pupils are chasing teachers. No-one wants to tell the simple truth: indiscipline.'

'Whoever dishes up a political slogan is a chief, and there are too many chiefs,' Mr Mazwai said.

Leaders called for peace but they didn't go to the ground to work for it. 'They only want a peace that leaves their organisation in a dominant position.' Mr Mazwai said the PAC/ANC peace talks were in tatters.

Helen Suzman: *I wonder what the devil I've been doing for 36 years. Has nothing been done to mobilise the vast majority of people who want stable lives? Is there no way journalists can mobilise that opinion? We seem totally intimidated and overcome by activists who are in the minority. The only person who put it bluntly was Motlana: intimidatory anarchy.*

Nomavenda Mathiane replied that it was not up to the journalists alone. Liberals also had a role: to question the activists. 'No-one asks the activists, what are you people about?'

Mr Nyatsumba said, in reply to Mrs Suzman's question, that a powerful minority called the tune in the townships, and it was dangerous to oppose it. But he also felt white liberals could make a contribution. They had been very vocal in their criticism of the government, 'but whenever the MDM was involved, or whenever there were necklaces, people have tended to condemn these in their bedrooms, in private, but they would not come public and condemn these things and question the leaders of these organisations.' Liberals should be asked to be more involved, to fight as vigorously for their values now as they had fought against the National Party government. 'That is the role that they can play and they can make a difference in that regard.'

10. WHAT'S TO BE DONE?

JOHN KANE-BERMAN

Executive Director, South African Institute of Race Relations

Dr Mogoba says that this audience has been shocked by what it has heard today. I am very glad to hear it: that was the intention. People who work in this building, Institute staff, have been hearing this story over and over again for the last three or four years, especially the intimidation of black journalists to stop them doing their jobs properly and giving members of the public the information they need. We felt it was time to persuade some of those who have been telling us these things privately, to say them to a wider audience.

The question that has been raised is, 'What's to be done?' This seminar is part of the answer — making the information we have been given today more widely available.

One of the Institute's strategies in its 61 years of existence has been to deal with problems by exposing them. Whether it was the iniquities of bantu education or the pass laws, or housing backlogs, or forced removals, or deaths in detention, we have always exposed things to the light of day in the hope that through greater public awareness, more people would be sensitised to the issue and take some sort of action about it.

One or two people here have asked why there have been no ANC journalists present, and in case others have a similar question, perhaps I should try and answer it. The reason is that the speakers who were invited here were not intended to be politically representative. All these people have over varying lengths of time been telling us what they've told you today. In a sense they chose themselves, because these are the people that have come and shared this information with us. They are the people who have been talking about these kinds of things, and few other people have been talking about them. We simply wanted them to talk to a wider audience than they've spoken to until now. Secondly, we decided quite deliberately that it was necessary to expose our membership to what I think may be termed, in the genuine sense of that word, alternative information. That is not only the question of coercive

63

violence but the fact that the media, as far as I can make out over four or five years now, have not been adequately reporting the extent of the violence taking place in the black community.

Let me give you an example, from various newspaper reports this very day. If you are a reader of *Business Day* and only of *Business Day*, you will have read a report this morning, about eight column inches, under the headline 'Protest March Halts Business', to the effect that there was 99% worker support for a stayaway called by various organisations in Bloemfontein yesterday. This is the essence of the report, that 99% of workers heeded the call for a stayaway. If your information was from the *Sowetan* rather than *Business Day*, you would find a report that was not referred to at all in *Business Day*, to the effect that a white security guard was shot and wounded in the neck during the course of the stayaway, and that the shot came from the crowd. The *Sowetan* goes on to say that 'several firms had large-scale absenteeism as workers feared for the safety of their homes after the houses of people who had tried to go to work were stoned. Staff who did get through the barricades were fearful of what they would find when they returned home later. The township roads were littered with stones and other obstacles as groups of youths gathered to ensure that workers heeded the ANC-UDF-COSATU alliance's call for a massive stayaway to protest the continued detention of its leaders, including leaders of the South African Communist Party.'

So one paper, the *Sowetan* — and it's a courageous thing it's been doing over quite a long period of time — is bringing out the fact that coercion was used in the stayaway in Bloemfontein. However this was completely ignored by the newspaper that the business community in South Africa relies on principally for its information.

We wanted to expose people, our membership, to the kind of information that we believe is not getting into the press. Let me give you another example. I don't know how many people present saw a little item in a number of Johannesburg newspapers this week, a paragraph or two, to the effect that several hundred people have been murdered by the necklace method over the past few years. You can bet that if this many people had been shot in the back by the police over the same period, it would have been front-page headlines in every newspaper in South Africa. It would no doubt have made the front pages of most foreign newspapers, and would have been on prime-time BBC, and all the American television networks as well. Yet the figures of necklace murders were almost buried by the bulk of the South African press.

I can't help suspecting that there's almost a racist dimension to this, in the sense that if the police misbehave they are part of the white government and their behaviour must be exposed and criticised in the media, but that if black people kill one another by necklacing, that somehow doesn't need condemnation or exposure by white-owned newspapers, because in a sense that is what black people can be expected to do, and after all black life is cheap.

An aspect of the problem that we face, I think, was correctly alluded to by Nomavenda Mathiane, when she talked about the role of white liberals. This constituency has a major say in the way in which newspapers in this country cover events. White liberals have an important part in shaping public debate, yet it seems to me that many such people are now very reluctant indeed to be as vigilant about threats to civil liberty from the left of the political spectrum as they were honourably vigilant about threats from the government or from right-wing organisations. It seems that a section, at any rate, of the liberal constituency has in fact abdicated its responsibilities.

Part of the liberal constituency is the Institute's own traditional constituency, and one of the ways in which we can attempt to address the problems highlighted here today is to stimulate greater awareness in that particular constituency.

Walter Saunders commented from the floor that revolutionary politics is solidarity politics. It seems to me that there is a fundamental difference between liberal politics and solidarity politics. The latter may also be termed totalitarian politics.

It is not new to this country. It wasn't so long ago that the National Party had to have its own Boy Scout organisation, so that when Nats got together to tie knots or make camp fires they had to do so as the Voortrekkers. It was not enough that there was a Red Cross, there had to be a National Party wing of the Red Cross, so they set up the Noodhulpliga. One could no doubt find a whole lot of other organisations that were all within the National Party camp.

This approach is characteristic of totalitarian parties, whether on the left or the right. They try to extend the domain of politics into every nook and cranny of national life. We have heard highlighted this afternoon the question of cultural desks, and reference also to academic boycotts and teachers' associations, but it happens in many other spheres too.

It happened recently in regard to bursaries, when a 'democratically accountable' association of scholarship-administering organisations was mooted. We were asked to join it. But we refused. This Institute recognises that in administering a bursary programme we are responsible to the donors to do it honestly and properly, to the students to pay the university fees on time, and to our own consciences to make fair selections and run the operation in an efficient way. We were damned if our bursary programme was in any way accountable to any kind of political organisation. So I want to suggest that one way in which the kind of pressures that are exerted by cultural boycotts and selective boycotts can be resisted is simply to resist them, to refuse to bow to that kind of pressure.

We have seen pressures in other fields. Five or six months ago every single one of you had an envelope addressed to you inviting you to a lecture in this hall on a Sunday night in March this year, by a Russian guest of the Institute. We were going to post these invitations, but we pulped them all, because this man arrived in South Africa too nervous to speak in public. The reason was that when the ANC's embassy in Moscow discovered that he was visiting South Africa (and doing so, as they said, behind their backs, without their permission), the Russian foreign ministry, as well as the Central Committee of the Communist Party of the Soviet Union, were brought in to stop him coming to South Africa, and he cancelled his visit. At the last minute he phoned me from Harare and said he was prepared to come if I could guarantee his personal safety. I said, 'Of course I can guarantee your personal safety, me and my ten battalions, come!' So he came, and he explained to us that his life and those of his family in Moscow had been threatened if he came to South Africa without seeking the permission of this particular political organisation. So it's not only in the cultural field that this kind of thing happens.

The South African Institute of Race Relations is a non-profitmaking organisation seeking to foster non-violent processes of change towards democracy in South Africa. It has no party political affiliations. Membership is open to all, irrespective of race, colour, creed, nationality, or country of residence.

The occasional publications listed elsewhere in this book are supplemented by *Quarterly Countdown* and *Social and Economic Update* (published every four months) and the annual *Race Relations Survey*.

If you would like to join the Institute and/or receive regular copies of our publications please write to the Membership Manager, South African Institute of Race Relations, P O Box 31044, 2017 Braamfontein.